SEL **Y**

27
MOMENTS
OF REFLECTION

RST-GENERATION

EMPOWERMENT

GRADUATE

EVINGERLEAN D. B. HUDSON, PH.D.

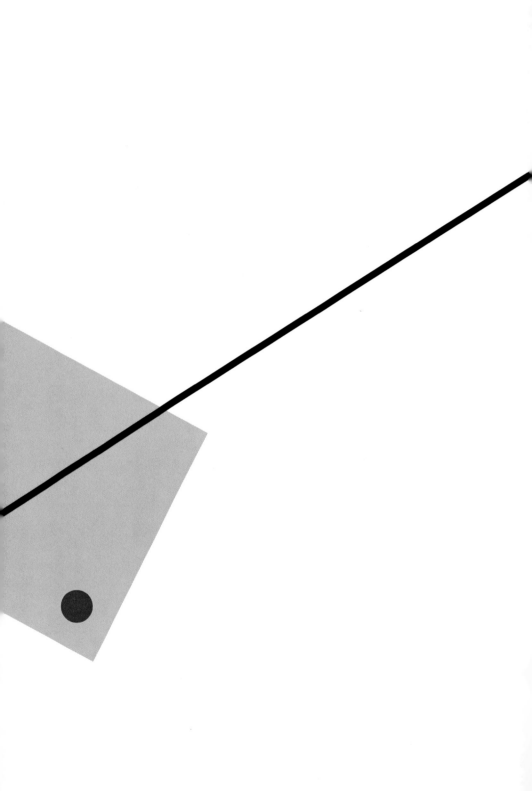

Journals may be purchased in bulk for promotional,
educational, or business use. Please send an email to
letschat@evingerleanworldwide.com for more
information.

ISBN-10: 0-9996418-2-4
ISBN-13: 978-0-9996418-2-8

First Printing May 2021

Published by
Evingerlean Worldwide Limited Liability Company
Charlotte, North Carolina, USA

TO THE TRA1LBLAZERS, HISTORY MAKERS, AND GAME-CHANGERS.
BE INSPIRED, EMPOWERED, AND UPLIFTED IN ALL THAT YOU DO!

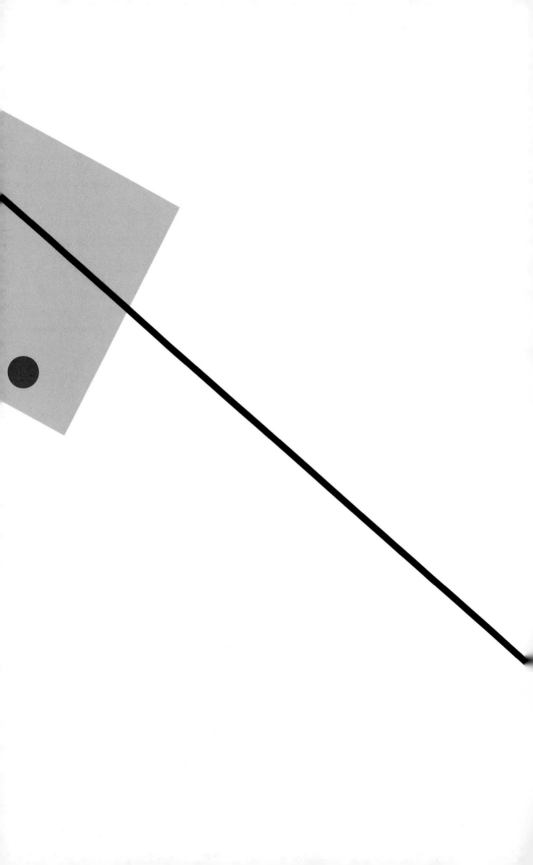

Hey, Fellow First-Gen College Grad!

As I was the first person in my family to get a college education, I remember feeling like I had "made it." (I know you know the feeling, right?) While I knew that this was a big accomplishment, and I was ready to take on the world, I had absolutely no idea how this first-gen identity was going to shape my life. In fact, I wouldn't have guessed in a million years that empowering fellow first-gens would become my life's work.

Anywho, considering the path I've traveled as a first-generation college graduate (FGCG) (and trust me when I say there've been many bumps on the road), I wanted to be able to reach back and help others along the way. So, I created this journal for you, as it is my greatest hope that you continue to own your life and trust that of which is inside of you.

No one knows your story better than you do. No one else will ever have the honor of being you. So do you, be you, and love you.

Before I go, I want to let you know this journal doesn't have a specific order, nor do you have to do it in a certain amount of time. Go as fast or as slow as you want to go. The most important thing is that you really reflect and "take it all in."

Aight now. Keep pressing forward!

XO.

Dr. Eve

I AM A TRA1LBLAZER

What does it mean to me to be an FGCG? How has it shaped my life so far? What are some of the biggest lessons that I've learned? How will I continue to blaze the trail?

I AM IN
CHARGE OF HOW I FEEL

How do I want to feel? What are some of the thoughts that I can think to help support how I want to feel?

I AM
FEARLESS AND FLOURISHING

What is fear? How do I respond when I'm afraid? Deep down, what are the real reasons why I'm afraid? What's the worst thing that can happen if I face that of which I fear?

I AM
WORTHY OF SUCCESS

What does success mean to me? What are some of the things (academically, personally, and/or professionally) for which I aspire? Why are these things important to me?

I KNOW
WHAT I'M DOING

●

What were nine (9) times when I didn't feel like I knew what I was doing, but I did it and excelled, proving myself (and sometimes people around me) wrong? How did it make me feel then? How have these moments shaped my thoughts about my abilities now?

I HAVE ALL
THAT I NEED WITHIN ME

What are some of my limiting beliefs and thoughts? What does my inner voice/critic tell me? What do I have to say to all of these things to set them straight today?

I AM
ALIGNED AND GROUNDED

How does my life look and feel when I am aligned and centered? What can I do to ensure I remain centered at all times? In what ways can I create better boundaries to protect my peace and wellbeing?

WHAT HAPPENED WAS SUPPOSED TO HAPPEN.
WHAT WILL HAPPEN IS SUPPOSED TO HAPPEN.
IT IS ALL A PART OF YOUR JOURNEY IN LIFE.

-Evingerlean D. B. Hudson, Ph.D.

I AM
EXCELLENT WITH MY COINS

What does winning financially look like for me? What am I doing well when it comes to my money? What are the financial habits that I want to change?

I HAVE A
BEAUTIFUL COMMUNITY

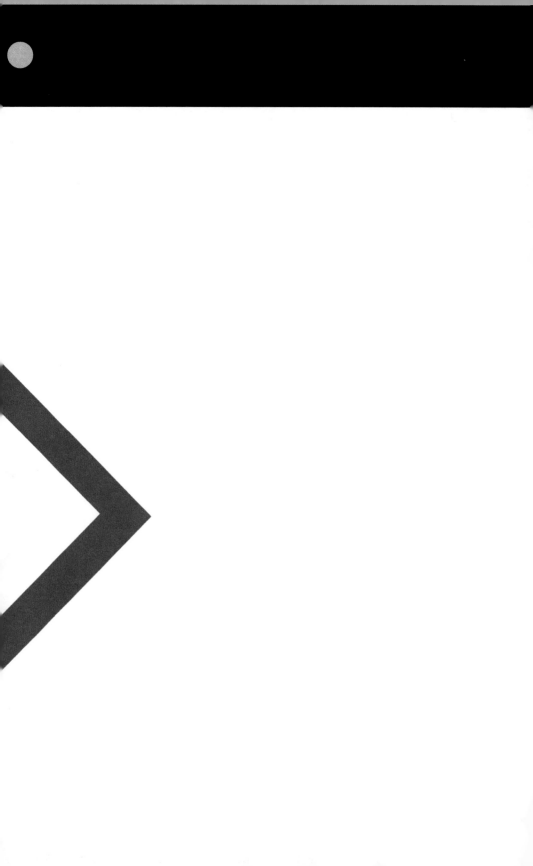

What is community to me? Who is a part of my community? How does my community add to my life? How do I invest in my community?

I TAKE CARE OF
MY MIND, BODY, AND SPIRIT

How do I recharge, rejuvenate, and renew my mind, body, and spirit?
What are some new ways of taking care of myself that I'd like to explore?
What can I commit to doing differently for the next 30 days?

I TAKE RESPONSIBILITY
FOR CREATING MY REALITY

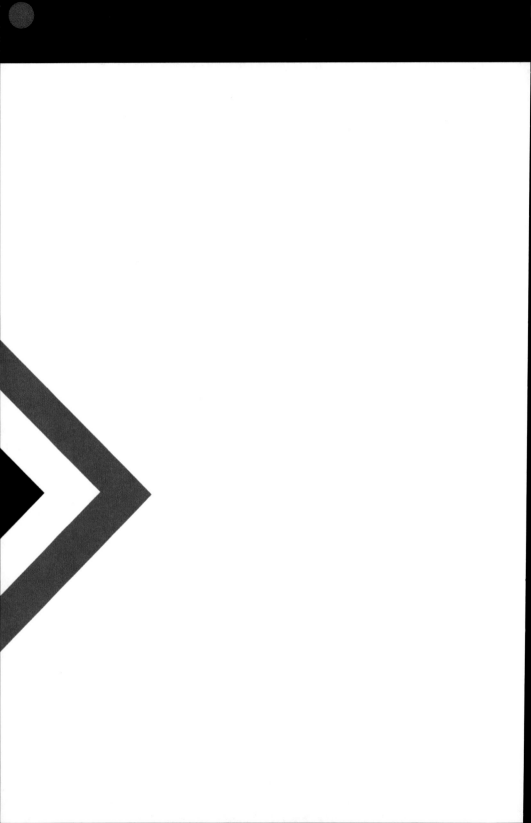

Why is it important for me to understand that it is me, and only me, who is responsible for my life? What can I do to continue to own my journey?

I ALWAYS
FIGURE THINGS OUT

How have the many challenges I've had to overcome shaped me? What have they taught me about problem solving? In what ways have they made me resourceful?

I BELONG
WHEREVER I MAY BE

What does it mean to me to belong? How do I respond when I feel like I don't belong? How can I take up space?

YOU ARE NOT YOUR CIRCUMSTANCES.
YOU ARE NOT YOUR PAST.
YOU ARE WHOEVER YOU DECIDE YOU WANT TO BE.

-Evingerlean D. B. Hudson, Ph.D.

I AM SAFE,
LOVED, AND PROTECTED

What are the things, and/or who are the people, that make me feel safe, loved, and protected?

I FOCUS
ON WHAT MATTERS MOST

What are my top nine (9) biggest priorities? Number one being my top priority. Am I content with how I'm spending my time? What are the things I can do differently/take off my plate because they are not a priority?

I AM
IN LOVE WITH MY LIFE

●

What are all of the things that I absolutely love about my life? Why do I love these things so much? What in my life do I want to be more in love with?

I AM OPEN
AND RECEPTIVE TO CHANGE

How do I deal with change? What do I find hard to change? Why? How can I embrace change more? What are some of the changes I want to make in my life?

I AM
WORTHY OF TRUST

What does it mean to me to be trustworthy? What are some of the decisions that I've made to show myself that I trust myself? In what areas of my life do I want to trust myself more?

I AM
BECOMING BETTER EACH DAY

How do I know when I have grown? In what ways have I grown, personally and professionally, over the past five (5) years? Past year? Past week? In what ways can I continue to invest in my development?

I RELEASE WHAT
IS OUT OF MY CONTROL

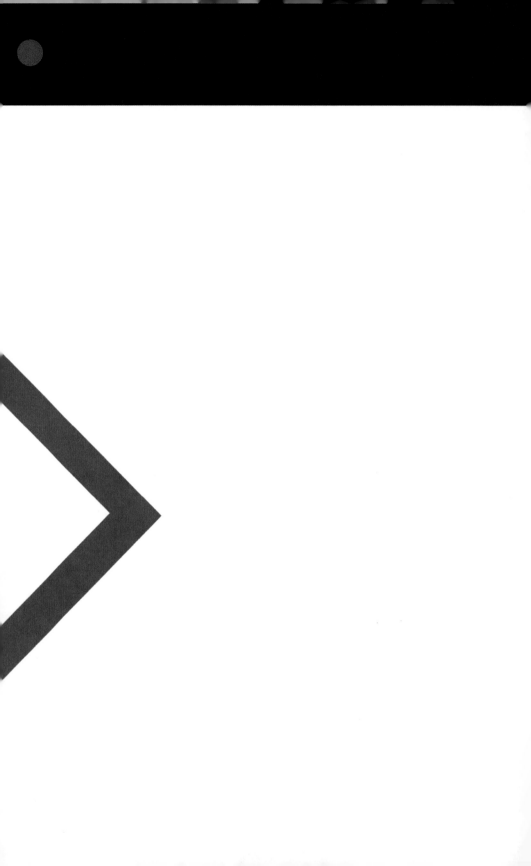

How do I respond to situations for which I have no control? What are the benefits of letting go of trying to control what I cannot? What do I recognize that is totally within my control?

I WILL GET ALL
THAT I WANT OUT OF LIFE

If I knew that there were no barriers and/or limitations, what would I want for my life? If time and money were unlimited, how would I live?

I AM
POWERFUL AND VALUABLE

What is it that makes me powerful and valuable? How can I continue to affirm that I am powerful and valuable each day? What are things that I can do to help those around me feel powerful and valuable, too?

I AM ENOUGH
AND FULLY ACCEPT MYSELF

27 facts about me AND a love letter to myself.

DON'T EVER DOUBT YOUR WORTH OR QUESTION IF YOU ARE VALUABLE.
TRUST THAT WHAT YOU WANT IN THIS LIFE IS YOURS.

-Evingerlean D. B. Hudson, Ph.D.

OVER AND ABOVE

YOU'VE HAD 27 MOMENTS TO REFLECT, **LEARN, AND BRING MORE AWARENESS** OF YOURSELF TO YOURSELF. SO, IF YOU'RE UP FOR THE CHALLENGE, HERE ARE A FEW BONUSES FOR YOU. **TAKE YOUR TIME.**

What are at least five (5) of the most significant things that I've learned about myself? How do I plan to respond to these new ideas? What are some of my new ways of thinking?

What are at least five (5) of the most significant things that I've learned about myself? How do I plan to respond to these new ideas? What are some of my new ways of thinking?

What and/or who is it that motivates and inspires me the most? Why? How will I continue to stay encouraged on this journey of mine?

What is the advice that I would like to give to my future self? What are the things that I need to remember? What do I want to be most proud of years from now?

How do I define legacy? What will it look like for me to leave my legacy? How am I working toward leaving my legacy each day?

FREE FLOW

ABOUT THE CREATOR

I am Evingerlean D. B. Hudson, Ph.D., affectionately known as Dr. Eve, and always excited to tell people that I'm a native of Charlotte, North Carolina. As the oldest of three reared by a single mother in a low-socioeconomic household, I went on to become a first-generation college student who eventually earned a Ph.D. at the age of 28.

While my first love and background is higher education, pursuing my purpose led me to social entrepreneurship and giving birth to Evingerlean Worldwide—an entity specializing in personal transformation and entrepreneurial development for first-generation college students and graduates.

I hold degrees from Shaw University (the oldest HBCU in the South) and The University of Southern Mississippi, and I'm a member of both alumni associations. I am also a very proud member of Delta Sigma Theta Sorority, Incorporated. I find joy in mentoring, traveling, reading, trying new foods, and engaging in research. I think cuddles with my chocolate lab, Maxwell Alexander Hudson, are the absolute best ever. I adore spending quality time with my best friend and life partner, Dr. James M. Hudson. (He's an HBCU alumnus and first-generation college graduate, too.)

A person I am most inspired by is my mommy, Norma J. Blakney, for she's one of the strongest and most courageous people I know. I can't think of a better person to have brought me into this world. I'm truly grateful that she's always given me the best that she's had to give and allowed me the space to figure out my life. To date, she continues to push me to follow my dreams and supports me every step of the way.

On that note, seeing that I love to meet my people (that includes YOU), I want for us not to be strangers. So, let's get connected. I invite you to find me by using the following handle
@evehudsonphd on social media platforms.

HAVE YOU HEARD OF THE FIRST-GEN LOUNGE?

The First-Gen Lounge (formerly The Purpose University Podcast) is the FIRST podcast of its kind—highlighting the experiences of first-gens. It's a place where we, first-generation college graduates, come to kick it and talk honestly about this thing called life and entrepreneurship.

It is here where YOU find community—we're people who break barriers and defy the odds but understand there is still much ahead of us; therefore, leaning on, and learning from, each other is what we do. In this space, we all belong and will uplift, inspire, and empower one another by sharing our truth as we tell our stories.

Be sure to check out the latest session of The First-Gen Lounge at www.evehudsonphd.com/lounge.

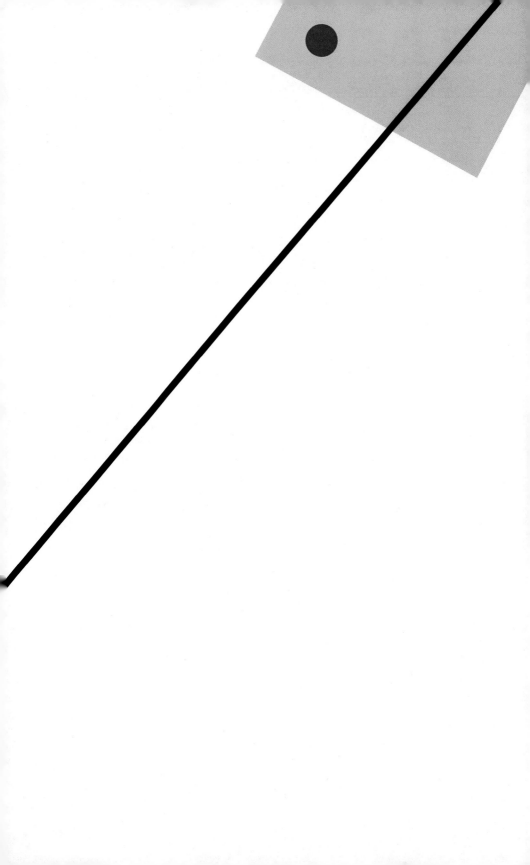

OVERCOME

GROW

BRAVERY

CONFIDENT

BE INSPIRED

Made in the USA
Middletown, DE
02 August 2023